THE BULLY INCOGNITO

Jarren Harrell

The Bully Incognito

Trilogy Christian Publishers

A Wholly Owned Subsidary of Trinity Broadcasting Network

2442 Michelle Drive, Tustin, CA 92780

For information, address Trilogy Christian Publishing

Rights Department, 2442 Michelle Drive, Tustin, CA 92780.

Trilogy Christian Publishing/ TBN and colophon are trademarks of Trinity Broadcasting Network.

For information about special discounts for bulk purchases, please contact Trilogy Christian Publishing.

Trilogy Disclaimer: The views and content expressed in this book are those of the author and may not necessarily reflect the views and doctrine of Trilogy Christian Publishing or the Trinity Broadcasting Network.

10 9 8 7 6 5 4 3 2 1

Library of Congress Cataloging-in-Publication Data is available.

ISBN 979-8-89333-896-6

ISBN 979-8-89333-897-3

DEDICATION

I want to dedicate this book first to my husband, Vann, who encouraged me to publish my writing even when I was reluctant. And to my daughters Sarah and Piper. You three are God's biggest blessing in my life. I love you. I also want to dedicate this to my parents, John and Debbie Grayson. Because of their love, I have never doubted that I can do anything God calls me to do. They are my biggest fans.
I love you, Mom, and Dad!

TABLE OF CONTENTS

INTRODUCTION

The other day I left my cell phone at home. It almost ruined my morning. I don't know why. I lived the first twenty-one years of my life without one. I am used to having it now, and I feel like I need it to make it through the day. I don't think it is the actual telephone I use as much as the immediate access to information whenever I need it. In today's world, we are so reliant on it. I am at the end of the Gen X generation. I am old enough to remember a time not so inundated by technology, but young enough that now I use it all the time. Aren't voice-activated commands so convenient? "Alexa. What's the weather?" Or "Siri. Find a pizza place near me." Just like that, our wish is AI's command. With just the spoken word, we have access to a ton of information in our homes and cars, all in the palm of our hand. The advancements in technology seem to come daily.

I was recently reading through the book of John, and it got me thinking. While I read the first few verses of chapter one, I slowed down a little. I looked at some highlights.

> *In the beginning was the Word, and the Word was with God, and the Word was God. He was with God in the beginning. Through Him all things were made; without Him, nothing was made that has been made. In Him was life and that life was the light of all mankind... The Word became flesh and made his dwelling among us... We have seen His glory, the Glory*

of the one and only Son, who came from the Father full
of grace and truth.

John 1:1–4, 14

John is the fourth gospel in the New Testament. It is a firsthand account of the life of Jesus. John is an eyewitness account. Today, historians would call that a primary source. He was there while Jesus walked the earth. John presents Jesus to us right away, but notice he does not call him Jesus. What does he call the Son of God? The Word! We are used to hearing words like Messiah, Savior, Rabbi, and Lord, but referring to Jesus as the Word is unique and catches my attention. John uses the Greek word "logos" in the original language and text. Britannica says it means "word," "reason," or "plan."[1] Greek philosophers and early Christian theologians refer to it as the divine ordering of the cosmos, giving it meaning and order. According to the Wycliffe Bible Commentary, those living in John's time would have understood that the word "logos" implied "concepts of wisdom, power and a special relationship with the Lord."[2] John reminds us that in the beginning, the Word was there. Not only was the Word "with God," but the Word "was God." It seems to me that the terms Word, God, and Jesus can be used interchangeably. It is like they are synonymous.

Look back at Genesis and the creation of the world. Genesis tells us that God spoke things into existence. He said it, and so it was. I cannot help but think that it is no coincidence that God created by speaking, and John reminds us that even before the beginning, "the Word" (Jesus—the Son) was there with God. John says the Word is God. In verse fourteen it says, "The Word became flesh and dwelled among us." There is power in the Word of God. That means there is power in the Bible because the Bible is God's Word. Taming the tongue is such a difficult feat. It requires power. Power that we don't have on our own. I have given much thought to words and taming the

THE BULLY INCOGNITO

tongue over the last several years. That is why I am writing. Let's rely heavily on Scripture for guidance and help. Through God's power, we can change.

What Is the Bully Incognito?

The tongue is an amazing part of our body. Just think about it. It is the only group of muscles that operates independently from the skeleton. It may not be the strongest muscle in the body, but it is strong and doesn't tire easily. Just think about all the eating and talking that you do all day. The tongue gets quite a workout. It is small and has no bones, but is as strong and damaging as any other part of us. I don't know about you, but I know some of us who can probably wreak more havoc with words than with a fist.

For my day job, I am a middle school teacher. I have concluded that kids can be very mean. I have taught many different ages of children over the years. It is much the same all around; kids make fun of kids, and they are ruthless. Bullying has become a buzzword in education over the years. However, as I took a closer look, I realized that our kids are learning from us, and bullying is not a kid or a school problem. One day I was waiting in the checkout line with my two daughters and witnessed incredibly rude behavior by the lady in front of me. She went off on the cashier and delivered her a verbal lashing throughout the entire duration of her checkout. That was when I realized we have a huge problem with this "bully incognito."

"Sticks and stones may break my bones, but words will never hurt me." Right? A childish "comeback" that for me is untrue. It is a little more accurate to say that sticks and stones may break my bones, but words can crush my spirit. Hurtful words stick with us. I know some people believe we are in control of whether we let hurtful words affect us. I respect and agree with that to some extent. I think it is fair to say that even those who wear that ultra-thick skin know deep down that words hurt. If I were a gambling gal, I would wager everyone reading is hanging onto a painful memory of a time when words hurt them.

What does "bully incognito" mean? Why did I choose those words? It is simple. Our words are the bully in disguise. Most of us do not consider ourselves bullies. I would agree that the average person is not a bully. However, I would argue that our words daily may be the source of hard feelings, anger, marital discord, and many other issues we face. Today, it is common to witness road rage, altercations at the gas pump, or any number of other verbal exchanges. There can be many reasons for us to get upset throughout the day. Somebody may pull out in front of us, mess up our food order, or leave their trash cans sitting in the front yard after trash day. We expect other people to live up to the standards society has put in place, and by golly, if they step out of line or inconvenience us in any way, we are going to let them hear it.

Scrolling through social media makes it easy to see that this "bully incognito" is alive and well. It runs rampant in our newsfeeds. Many of us have grown accustomed to it and even participate in it. We grow belligerent and unkind when someone does not agree with us. We spew opinions of all kinds like they are the gospel truth and berate those who do not fall in line with the way we see the world. By "we," I mean society. Now I admit that social media is somewhat of a soapbox for me. I won't stay there long. Social media can be a problem that leads to anger, broken relationships, and hard feelings. This is something I have given much thought and consideration to.

I believe what the Bible says is true, so many of my ideas and thoughts are based on principles I have read and learned from God's Holy Word. I realize that will make some of you not want to read the book, but I encourage you to stick with me. I believe the Bible is God's inspired and infallible Word. That means there are no mistakes there, and it comes straight from God. If you have never read the Bible, I recommend reading the book of John for starters.

We will look to Scripture often while talking about the importance of our words. The book of Matthew records the very words of Jesus. Matthew is another firsthand witness to the life of Jesus and wrote many of His lessons down for us to read. In the book of Matthew, Jesus gives us a very clear picture of why it is important to be careful with our words. The following verses probably do the best job of summing up the reasons I have begun writing about this "bully incognito."

> *Make a tree good and its fruit will be good, or make a tree bad and its fruit will be bad, for a tree is recognized by its fruit. You brood of vipers, how can you who are evil say anything good? For the mouth speaks what the heart is full of. A good man brings good things out of the good stored up in him, and an evil man brings evil things out of the evil stored up in him. But I tell you that everyone will have to give account on the day of judgment for every empty word they have spoken. For by your words you will be acquitted, and by your words you will be condemned.*
>
> Matthew 12:33–37

There is so much to be learned from these verses, but for now, just take a minute to think about them. The thing that hit home to me was that we will be held accountable for our words. They will acquit or condemn us. That is a sobering thought to me. How many times have I vented in a moment of emotion or joked, thinking it was no big deal? It all matters. There is more to talk about in this scripture, but I will wait until later to dive in deeper.

Words are important. There is a part of me that hasn't wanted to write this book because I know I am flawed, just like everyone else. I also think if we focus on what the Bible has to say about our words, we cannot go wrong. I want to walk this journey together. Join me as we explore some ways to help us be better stewards of our words as we journey through life. I am sorry to say that I do not claim to have mastered the controlled tongue. Although I work on it daily. I do hope to bring this problem of the "bully incognito" to your attention while offering suggestions and hope as we strive to live for the Lord.

May we speak life into the people around us as easily as we use voice commands to access information or control our creature comforts. I truly believe we can speak life and healing into those around us. It may not come naturally, but with God's help and power, we can do it.

Chapter 1

---∞---

THE PROBLEM

If you have not read *The Five Love Languages* by Gary Chapman, I highly recommend it.[3] It is eye-opening. We all give and receive love differently. My love language is words of affirmation. For me, words matter a lot. Including the tone and manner in which they are delivered. Ironically, I have a quick tongue and work hard to curb it. It matters how we talk to each other. Our words show more about us than we would like to admit.

A problem I have observed lately is a general attitude of aggression and hate. I am not even talking about politics or the media. We all know aggression and hate run rampant there. I am referring to everyday spaces. Our homes, workplaces, shopping centers, and, of course, social media. I'll talk more about social media in the next chapter, but I feel strongly that it is a breeding ground for all sorts of negative behavior. We can turn off the devices, and I would argue that many times we should. It is much harder to "turn off" the people we meet each day. We must manage the everyday annoyances without forgetting how we make other people feel. That is a tall order, I know!

It seems so easy to make someone mad. If the waitress brings the wrong food or does not fill our drinks...that's it. We are done. If customer service is poor, we complain to a manager, and you better not cut someone off in traffic because road rage is sure to follow. Sometimes anger is justified, but stop and think for a moment about the little things we let upset us that won't matter in a day or even an hour. Sometimes I expect perfection from those around me, even when I know that I am not perfect. Does anyone else do that?

Let's stick with the idea of traffic for a minute. I get irritated if I am running late and someone driving at a snail's pace pulls out in front of me, hindering my ability to hurry up. I am not a horn blower, and I do not show my road rage outwardly, but sometimes on the inside, I am ready to pop. Then one day I pulled out in front of someone, and they were not happy with me. There was much gesturing and honking. I immediately felt bad. I HATE being honked at. (That's probably why I don't use my horn.) I realized that I didn't purposely do it. Sure, I was probably distracted, and it was my fault, but I wasn't intending to cause harm or irritation to the other driver.

Now I try hard to show grace to other drivers, as I would have liked to have been shown that day. It is a simple example, I know, but the message is that if we take a minute to step back in situations that anger us, we may find the offender just needs a little grace. Their crime was nothing more than being an imperfect human being in a fallen world, something we are all guilty of. (See Romans 3:23.)

What does anger and aggression have to do with the bully incognito? A lot. The Bible tells us in Matthew 12:34 that "out of the overflow of the heart the mouth speaks" (BSB). In the introduction, we learned that this passage tells us we will be held accountable for the things we say. I look at it this way. We are good at putting on a good show. We fix our outward appearances, smile for the public, and follow social norms. However, you cannot cover up your character and the kind of person you are. It seeps out through your mouth in the form of words. I know I have put my foot in my mouth more times than I can count. The words come out, and I instantly wish I could take them back. How you talk reveals your true character. It is a sobering thought, if you ask me.

Now do not get me wrong. Anger is sometimes justified. Even Jesus became angry when the situation warranted it. The Bible tells us not to sin in our anger. I tell my kids that when they get mad at me, I am all right with that. They can be mad, but I also tell them that does not mean they can speak harshly or disrespectfully. Self-control comes into play when dealing with the aggravations of everyday life.

Why is it such a problem if we slip up and hurt someone with our words? I think it is a big problem because it can't be undone. Once the words are spoken, the damage is done. You cannot take it back. There is no redo. I was once reading about the damage caused when someone is exposed to radioactive material. The extent of the damage depends on two things. The first is obviously how *much* radiation a person is exposed to. The more they are exposed to, the more damage there will be. The second factor is how close in proximity the person was to the radiation. What a picture this creates if you think of it in the context of our speech. If our words are radioactive, the people closest to us will experience the most damage. In turn, the frequency and volume of our radioactive words directly correlate to the amount of damage done.

I can also give a more personal example. I suffer from moderate hearing loss. When I first discovered this, I sought out the help of doctors. I had surgery that was hopefully going to help with the hearing loss and prolong the time before I would need hearing aids. Things did not go as planned. My nerves were damaged during surgery. I could no longer move the right side of my face. It was a scary and devastating time in my life.

Fast forward a few months. I chose to see another doctor for a second opinion. I was told that the damage had already been done. There was no going back. There wasn't anything that could be done except to wait and see if the nerves would regenerate and pray for a miracle. The prognosis wasn't encouraging. After six months, there was a slight improvement and some movement was restored, but to this day, my face isn't the same, and I still can't move the right side of my face. The point of this story is that even accidents can be hard to come back from. Sometimes it is hard to restore the damage. Sure, my face improved, but the scars are still there.

After letting that sink in, be encouraged. There is forgiveness. We can be forgiven by our heavenly Father and hopefully by the loved ones we hurt along the way. Relationships survive mistakes all the time. What I am getting at is that wounds created by hurtful words can heal, but scar tissue will be left behind.

I look at my daughter's face and see a scar she got fifteen years ago as a toddler. The pain is long gone. The memory of that emergency room visit is not. I even remember the clothes I had on that night. (For me, that is a big deal. I am not always detail-oriented.) The images of the memory and how I felt that night will always be there somehow.

Much like physical wounds, emotional wounds come with stories to tell and scar tissue that is left behind as a reminder. Even though relationships heal after careless words, we must try not to do damage. If someone is learning to skateboard, we will encourage them to wear protective gear. Just in case. There will be injuries, and most everyone falls while learning to do an activity like skateboarding. It is a part of life. That does not mean we don't try to lessen the damage. I see it the same way with relationships and other people. Feelings will get hurt. It is unavoidable. Don't just throw in the towel and quit because you mess up sometimes. Keep striving to improve. Every hurtful word that stops before it leaves the lips is a success. Celebrate it and learn from it.

Chapter 2

---◇◇---

THE WAR ZONE

I titled this chapter "The War Zone" because I am constantly observing situations where it seems as if people are in a verbal "war," so to speak. It is a classic battle. Lines are crossed, tempers flare, sides are taken, and casualties result. The saddest war zone is our home. The place where our family is. Our sanctuary from the world. I don't know about you, but I have noticed that, sadly, I can often exhibit more self-control out there in the world than I can under my own roof. It is like this unexplainable phenomenon.

For example, those days when you are reading the riot act to your kids for not doing their homework, and then a friend calls. You do a one-eighty and change your tone of voice. We can't let the person on the other end of the phone hear us talking that way. Yet we can let our family soak it up regularly. Does anyone else experience this phenomenon in their home? I have a feeling it isn't just me. We are comfortable at home. We let our hair and our defenses down, and then it just sort of happens. At least that is the way it is for me.

As I said before, I am a teacher. There are days when I feel like I will scream if someone calls my name one more time. I literally might explode. Those days are not very often, thank goodness, but they appear. The thing is, I come home to my family every day after work. They need things too. If you are a working parent, you know what I mean. "Mom, can I have a snack?" "Mom, can I watch TV?" "Mommy, can you get me some more toilet paper?" "What's for dinner, Mom?" "When will Dad be home?" The truth is that I love being a wife and mother and would have it no other way, but there are days when I feel like going into my room and hiding. (Sometimes I do. I highly recommend it for those intense days. A break helps.) It is understandable. I try very hard not to take frustrations out on my family. I don't always succeed. It isn't right that the outside world gets Mr. Hyde and then the people at home see Dr. Jekyll.

I am fascinated by the popularity and obsession with social media. I said before, it is a little bit of a soapbox for me, so I won't stay here long. I know that social media has some positive attributes. It seems the negative ones just outweigh them. I rarely post on social media, but I do scroll through it occasionally. It drives me crazy to see how mean people are to each other. This brings me to another war zone, if you will.

It is not hard to scroll through social media and see at least one mean-spirited post or response. Now we are not just mean or hurtful to people we know, but to strangers we have never seen before. A friend can share something on social media. Another one of their friends then responds with strong words because they disagree with what was said. Then along comes another friend, who tells the second friend how wrong and idiotic they are. It is a vicious cycle. If you post something to social media that your friends don't agree with, they will let you have it, and then strangers will join in on the fun.

Why do we feel the need to share our opinions...constantly? It is usually better to keep our thoughts to ourselves. It is all right with me if you don't agree with something I post on social media. That doesn't bother me in the least, but it seems like in this culture that is not the norm. People are not kind to those they don't see eye-to-eye with. What ever happened to "If you don't have something nice to say, don't say anything at all?"

If you lived through the coronavirus pandemic, I am sure you witnessed the daily verbal firestorms that resulted over a variety of topics. Health, politics, education, and many more hot topics easily stirred up anger and violent words. I had to sign off for a while and take a breath. For one, I am passionate and have strong opinions and feelings, just like many of you. On the other hand, I don't want to get caught up in the mess. Option one was to live with a constantly bleeding tongue (you know... from all the biting). Option two is to sign off, so the temptation to respond isn't there. I chose option two. I just quit scrolling, and I felt so much better.

Let's be honest. How many of us have changed our opinion or taken a different stance because of what someone posted online? I haven't, and my guess is that not many of you have either. I figure why risk responding and hurting someone when it is not going to change how they think anyway? To all my friends who enjoy social media for family pics and funny memes, there is a place for that too. It is good to remember that even when they are typed, our words count. They may even count a little more.

KIND AND NICE

Whether online or in person, social interactions can be tricky. As a Christian, I see many things I don't agree with. Things that don't align with God's Word. When do I open my mouth? When do I stay silent? It is hard to know and requires wisdom from the Lord.

Do you know what the difference is between nice and kind? I didn't. I never even thought about it, to be honest. Recently, I saw the idea that there is a difference between nice and kind spoken about three different times. It has stood out to me. The most recent occurrence was in church this past Sunday. I was fascinated as I listened to the pastor talk about being kind and nice and how

Christians should be kind, but that was not the same thing as nice. The definition of nice, according to Webster's Dictionary, is "pleasing or agreeable."[4] Other definitions used words like "pleasant" or "polite." Websters defined kind as having a sympathetic or helpful nature, a forbearing nature, or gentle.[5] Dictionary.com used words like benevolent, gentle, and humane.[6] The two words that stuck out to me the most were forbearing and gentle.

These are two fruits of the Spirit that I don't always come by so easily. Forbearance, or patience, stuck out to me because that is probably a prerequisite to kindness. Don't get me wrong. I am not suggesting that it isn't good to be nice. I just thought it was interesting that being kind is not necessarily the same thing. I had never thought about it that way. It is the idea that being kind is not necessarily always nice. There may be times for us to share Jesus that are not pleasant or nice for us or the other person. It is kind, though. Sharing the gospel truth is always kind.

We should stand firm while proclaiming Christ and standing for biblical principles. However, this doesn't mean we need to berate those we disagree with. Kindness is being honest about God's Word. Sometimes causing us to tell the hard truth. On the other hand, being nice is not ruffling feathers. We may not want to upset others and just prefer to be polite. We do not want to step on their toes if they see things differently. What a balancing act!

We are called to tell others about Jesus and God's forgiveness. In today's world, Christians are often seen as closed-minded or intolerant. For some of us, it makes us want to be nice. Just politely let them live their lives and don't openly disagree. Others want to scream it from the rooftops. In their zeal, and sometimes anger, they just want to shake the other person until they can get through to them. What if there was another way? Speak the truth. Don't water it down. Proclaim God's Word, but do not forget that if it isn't motivated by love, it probably won't be well received. Remember, the person on the other end of the conversation, whether virtual or face-to-face, is a human being and part of God's creation just like you. We can love them despite our disagreements, their sin, or our sins.

Chapter 3

---∞---

THE PLANK EYE PHENOMENON

Why is it so much easier to point out the faults in others rather than to look inside ourselves and see that we are the ones who need to change? The truth of the matter is that we cannot fix others. Even our most cherished loved ones have free will and cannot be controlled. How often do we try to change our spouse, kids, or even our friends?

The four gospels are full of Christ's teaching. He loved to teach with stories and parables. One is a story about a man with a plank in his eye. It is an excellent example of Jesus's teaching. He wastes no time and gets straight to the point.

> *Why do you look at the speck of sawdust in your brother's eye and pay no attention to the plank in your own eye? How can you say to your brother, "Brother, let me take the speck out of your eye," when you yourself fail to see the plank in your own eye? You hypocrite, first take the plank out of your eye, and then you will see clearly to remove the speck from your brother's eye.*
>
> Luke 6:41–43

I like these verses for the visual image they provide. Imagine walking around with a huge plank of wood protruding from your eye, and the only thing you are concerned about is this little speck of dust in someone else's eye. The thought of it is absurd (and humorous, I might add), but the point is simple. We are so quick to judge others and lash out verbally when someone does something that we, in our righteous indignation, disapprove of. One thing I have never understood is why people, me included, so readily pass judgment on others. I have always hated it when someone acts like they are better than somebody else. We are all human beings with feelings and lives that matter. End of story. People look down on others for all sorts of reasons. Maybe it is because of their race, religion, bank account, or landscaping skills (don't laugh, it is a real problem in some neighborhoods). It is human nature, but God's Word lets us know that we are not the judge, and we don't make the call as to who has value and who doesn't. Whew! Aren't you relieved? I mean, that is a huge weight to bear.

The second reason I like this verse is that Jesus holds no punches. Look again at what he calls the "plank eye" offender. "You hypocrite." Ouch, that is harsh. Nobody wants to think of themselves as a hypocrite. The fact of the matter is that we are all guilty of some wrongdoing at one time or another. Lucky for us, Christ came to earth born of a virgin, spent His time on earth teaching about love, and made the ultimate sacrifice while being nailed to a cross. This is important because it shows us where we stand. Without the sacrifice of Jesus, we are all doomed. No good deed, philanthropy, or moral high road will get us a spot in eternity with Jesus. Why? Because we all are sinners. Every single human being. No exceptions.

All right, now for the good news. All we need to do is accept that fact and acknowledge that Jesus is the only way to be forgiven. After we accept that fact, we confess it with our mouths and believe in Him. Then comes our eternal salvation. It is simply a gift, and we just need to open it.

What does all of this have to do with the "plank eye" phenomenon? It allows us to see that we are in no place to judge others. There is a judge, and we are not it. That is God's job. We can read the Bible, decipher its lessons and direction, and make morally sound decisions about right and wrong, but it is not for us to place judgment on another person. There are clear rights and wrongs in life, and it is all right to live your life by them and to even teach those lessons to those around you. That is why we need church, friends, and family. We all need encouragement and help when walking the straight and narrow.

What I am talking about is overstepping our bounds and being judgmental. I believe there is a difference between placing judgment on a single behavior or action and placing judgment on a person. It is just not our place to do that. In Matthew 7:2 it tells us, "Do not judge, or you too will be judged. For in the same way, you judge others you will be judged, and with the measure you use it will be measured to you." I think this sounds like a what goes around comes around type of situation. I can be so hard on other people sometimes. Expecting perfection from other imperfect human beings. When all along, I am messing up and making mistakes of my own. I imagine Mary Poppins with her tape measure. You know. The one that measures her as "practically perfect in every way." I see it like this. Whatever tape measure I use to judge others will be what is used to judge me. I am feeling a lot more lenient now!

One of my favorite authors is C.S. Lewis. He writes about forgiveness (and many other things) in his book, *Mere Christianity*.[7] In chapter seven, Lewis addresses the idea where Jesus says, "Love your neighbor as yourself" (Matthew 19:19). He also points out that the Bible tells us we must forgive others if we want to be forgiven (Matthew 6:15 and Colossians 3:13). Lewis writes that even though we know our own shortcomings and faults, we still love and care for ourselves. We give ourselves a whole lot more grace than we do other people. I know that when I mess up, I want a second chance.

I am not always so gracious with others. Sometimes our neighbors are our enemies. The people you encounter during the day are your neighbors, even if just for a moment in time. Lewis also suggests we don't always have to condone another's behavior or even like them to love and forgive them. Jesus set the example while walking the earth. Our job is to follow suit.

Here is the tricky part. What about those times when someone does something just plain wrong, and they deserve a little tongue-lashing to set them straight? I remember one time when my girls were young. While we were at the pool, there was this young boy who continued to bother my daughters the entire time we were there. It started by taking their toys right from their hands and progressed from there. My first reaction was annoyance, but I quickly instructed my girls to share the toys. After a little time passed, I made sure he gave them back. That worked for a little while. I was sitting on the side of the pool watching my youngest daughter jump into the water while her big sister "caught" her. It was priceless and fun to watch as their mom. The giggles, the splashing, the sunshine...it was good times despite the boy toy thief.

Then, low and behold, this kid, right in front of me, walks up and begins to push my little one into the pool. Thankfully, I was right there. My teacher's voice and mamma bear claws showed up all at once. I was able to stop him, but not for long. Before I could blink, his hands were on the back of my baby girl yet again. This time, I made myself known and told his mother. I was mad. His mother was right there, not five feet away. Why didn't she do something? Can't she see her son misbehaving? Is she even watching? It is times like these when a mom feels justified in jumping into the verbal boxing ring. Shouldn't I let her know how badly her son has been behaving the whole time? I certainly have the right to stand up for my kids.

This is the conclusion I came to. First, what you need to know is that the mother was nearby, but she was playing with this little boy's baby sister. It is possible she did not see. The second realization I had was that even though it was upsetting to watch, I was able to stop it. No harm done. The bottom line is that the girls were not bothered a bit, and, therefore, in the big picture, there was no need to put this other mom in her place. I guess the point I am trying to make with this unimportant example is that sometimes, in the moment, things seem like a much bigger deal than they are. If we can take a step back when our emotions kick in, it may help us to understand and respond to the situation in a better way.

Now there are times when we need to stand up for what is right. Just like I needed to stop that boy from pushing my daughter. However, many times we take it to the next level. It is not enough that we do the right thing. We want to also let the other person know how wrong they are while we are being so right.

My suggestion is that before you point out that speck of dust you see in your neighbor, consider if it is really necessary. Does it need to be said? Sometimes it does. Something needs to be said when the kid at school repeatedly bothers your child. When your boss is asking you to do something unethical, something needs to be said. When someone cuts in front of you in line at Target, something needs to be said. Oh, wait...maybe, just maybe, we let that one slide. You're in a hurry. I know. Is five minutes going to alter your day that much?

Slow down and think before you act and speak. Here is some great advice. "Everyone should be quick to listen, slow to speak, and slow to become angry" (James 1:19). Listen fast, talk less, and don't let anger creep in. The next part of that verse says, "Man's anger does not bring about the righteous life God desires." Getting angry is damaging to us and our relationships.

I am an impulsive person when it comes to my thoughts and words. It is something I try to change daily. Sometimes I feel like my words are quicker out of the mouth than Billy the Kid's pistol out of the holster. Firing bullets left and right without being "quick to listen" first. Then comes the damage. Feelings get hurt, anger leads to poor decision making, and the list goes on.

There is one more reason I like the "plank eye" passage from Matthew. There is a little nugget of wisdom packed into the tail end of verse 5. It is possible to remove the plank from your eye, and when you do, "then you will see clearly to remove the speck of dust from your brother's." That word "then" is powerful. It lets us know there is a sequential order to things. First, do this, and then do that. It is a natural progression. Before we take care of those around us who we think need to get their act together, we need to look inward first. Deal with our shortcomings; we all have them, and then we can be a blessing to others and help them rid their eye of that irritating little speck.

Although I must tell you that I feel that once you deal with your own plank, you won't be quite so concerned with the specks you see in the eyes of others. If we focus more on getting ourselves straight, we might care less about straightening out others. Please don't get me wrong. Jesus does tell us there are times when we can help clear the eyes of those around us. I am just cautioning that maybe our knee-jerk reaction to putting others in their place when they offend us is not always the best approach. Often, we can take a gentler path that allows us to step back and reflect on the situation rather than reacting. The adage "think before you speak" is applicable and helpful but admittedly hard to live by. We will make mistakes and more mistakes, but with practice, we can learn to focus on the important things and not the everyday annoyances.

Chapter 4

———∞———

THE GOLDEN RULE

Many of you grew up learning some form of the "Golden Rule" from your parents. It comes from Matthew 7:12, "So in everything, do to others what you would have them do to you, for this sums up the laws and the prophets." Even for those who do not practice religion or claim to be a person of faith, this is a well-known idea. Many cultures, religions, and people groups have their own versions. It simply means you should treat other people the way you would like to be treated. The problem is that this goes against our natural inclination to treat other people the way they deserve, or the way we *think* they deserve, according to their behavior.

When someone is kind to us or easy to be around, it is easier to reciprocate that same kindness and goodwill. The opposite also rings loud and clear. When a person is a bully, irritating, or just plain old difficult to be around, we feel we have the right to retaliate and give them a taste of their own medicine. I have tasted my own medicine before, and let me tell you, it doesn't taste good.

If you are a parent, you especially know what I am talking about. Our children are good at showing us how we behave and mess up. They are little carbon copies of us running around. Sometimes I look at my children and I see myself. The good and the bad are there. I appreciate it if people let it slide when I make a mistake.

Sometimes I will mess up, and my husband will get aggravated with me. Inside I am like, "Geez, I messed up. Give me another chance. Please?" Then I walk away and think about the other day when he messed up, and I didn't show him the grace I just asked for. Yikes! It is terrible, but true. Can anyone relate? Sometimes I want more grace and mercy than I am willing to give. When someone needs grace, I try to remember to let them have it because in a minute or two I am sure I will need the favor to be returned.

If you have a conversation about the" Golden Rule" with a child, it can be quite entertaining and frustrating at the same time. It will go something like this. "You really should not hit your classmates; you have to treat your friends the way you want to be treated." Then the child will say something like this: "He hit me first, so that must mean he wants me to hit him, and he is not my friend anyway." Next comes a slight smirk and a look of triumph because, after all, no adult can ever argue with that logic. Right? It can go on for some time as you try to explain to them that it doesn't work that way. You see, the "Golden Rule" isn't dependent on the other person. Did you catch that? It has nothing to do with what the other person says or does. I can hear some of you huffing as you read. I get it. I am human too, and it isn't easy. When we get hit, our instinct is to hit back. I mean, come on, they started it anyway.

Here is the thing. When we are reactionary, we are not in control. We are letting circumstances control us. If we base our actions on the behavior of others, we are giving them power over us. Kids love to say, "They made me do it." Nobody can make you do anything. Be in control. Take charge, and don't react too quickly.

We are in the wrong the minute we decide to retaliate or show someone else what it's like to be on the receiving end of their bad behavior. In that moment, we become the bad guy. Without even realizing it, we have mistreated someone. You took my parking spot! Well, I'm going to follow you into the store and give you an earful about having manners and being a better driver. Take that! You let your toy poodle do its business on my lawn? I will not only shovel it back where it belongs, but I will also train my two golden retrievers to make their mess in your yard. Take that! My daughter was not invited to the birthday party. That is all right. I will make sure yours is left out of every summer slumber party for years to come. Take that! We could play this game forever. Doesn't it sound so childish? These examples may seem silly, but if we were honest, I bet we have done or said at least one of them. The truth is that adults behave this way just on a grander scale because they have had more practice.

The last little line in Matthew 7:12 says, "And this sums up the law and the prophets." The law and prophets refer to the Old Testament. The Old Testament, while full of wonderfully rich stories and godly wisdom, is slammed full of rules and instructions. Guess what? Jesus just told us that we can sum all of them up in one little principle. Treat others the way you want to be treated. Plain. Simple. Imperative sentence. An imperative sentence gives an instruction. Go wash the dishes. Please call me before you leave. Don't forget our date tonight. These are not statements, questions, or exclamations. They are directives, and so is Matthew 7:12.

REAPING AND SOWING

Another concept like the Golden Rule is reaping and sowing. The world says it in many ways. Some call it karma or say, "What goes around comes around." The Bible refers to it as reaping and sowing. These terms are related to agriculture. You sow the seed and reap the harvest. We can "sow" many things in life. We can "sow" resources, like time and money. We can "sow" our talents. We can "sow" our attitude and words. The more of something you sow, the bigger the harvest will be.

The apostle Paul says it like this: "A man reaps what he sows. Whoever sows to please their flesh, from the flesh will reap destruction; whoever sows to please the Spirit, from the Spirit will reap eternal life. Let us not become weary in doing good, for at the proper time we will reap a harvest if we do not give up" (Galatians 6:7–9).

If we sow kindness with our words, then that is what we will reap. The hard part is that there is a time lapse between the sowing and the reaping. The harvest is not always immediate. You need to wait. I think that is why Paul tells us not to grow weary. We like quick results. Our culture has taught us to seek instant gratification. It is hard to have patience.

It is hard to live by the Golden Rule and treat others the right way when they are not doing the same thing. It is even harder when we live by biblical principles and the results are not instantaneous. They do work. The harvest will come. Start with something simple. The next time someone mistreats you, try responding the opposite way your human nature wants you to. Being calm when the other person is ranting and angry has amazing results. It is hard to argue or keep yelling at someone who responds with quietness and kindness. When tensions rise and you stay calm, it helps to disarm the other person. The expectation is for us to rise to their level of anger. When they don't get the desired result, it gets their attention. Of course, there are always outliers and exceptions, but most of the time the situation deescalates.

Proverbs 15:1 says, "A gentle answer turns away wrath." That is exactly what we are going for. By being gentle and not angry, we are changing the direction of the conversation. Who knows? Maybe the discord and anger will make a turn for the better. King Solomon tells us it will "turn away wrath." It will redirect the situation. That is exactly what we need when things get heated.

The bottom line is that we can only control our responses. We can't change other people. That is not our job. We can change us, with God's help. Taking the time to think about how we should treat and talk to others is a good place to start. Just do not leave out the Lord. I have tried taming my tongue with simple willpower. Trust me when I tell you it does not work well. We are going to need supernatural help.

Chapter 5

---∞---

THE LITMUS TEST

Do you remember using the litmus test in chemistry class to see if a substance was an acid or a base? So simple, but important in the lab! The test for our words can be equally simple. It comes down to one question. Is what I am about to say helpful? It is that easy. Easy may not be the best choice of words. It will often be the very opposite of easy. Let us just say it is that simple. There are no complicated formulas. One yes-or-no question can provide all the information you need to know when determining if what you are thinking should come out of your mouth.

I think it would be helpful if words could be on some sort of verbal fishing line you could conveniently reel back in should they escape unwantedly. It can be difficult to take the time to think before you speak, which is what it takes to apply this test. Ephesians 4:29 says, "Do not let any unwholesome talk come out of your mouth, but only what is helpful for building others up according to their needs that it may benefit those who listen." I love how Scripture does not leave us hanging. It could have just told us to watch what we say and be careful with our words. Nope. Paul, the author of Ephesians, includes some help.

The second part of the verse lets us know how to tell if what we are about to say is acceptable. Does it build others up? Does it benefit them? Words that pass the litmus test are good to go. Words that do not pass should stay put. This is no easy rule to live by. You will probably fail at times. I do! Why even bother? Let me tell you why. If we do not at least attempt to think first and speak later, if we do not judge our words by their usefulness, then we stay a part of the problem rather than the solution. We live in a fallen world where people make mistakes constantly. We are human, and not one of us is exempt from this imperfectness.

Don't be discouraged, though, because we are not supposed to be perfect. The Lord only asks us to let His power work through us. We do not have the power to be perfect with our speech, nor can we take back our words after they float past our lips. That is where faith comes in. If Jesus lives in you, He is made strong where you are weak. I am oh so weak in this area. I love to jump in the verbal boxing ring with the best of them, especially when provoked. That is why it took me a while to write this book. How could I encourage others when it is such a struggle in my own life?

Then I remembered Moses, one of the most famous Old Testament heroes, who confronted Pharaoh and led Israel out of Egypt. Moses was guilty of murder and ran. When God called him, he resisted because he felt inadequate and was not a good public speaker. Moses obeyed and brought God's people out of slavery so they could enter the land promised to them. To me, that is proof that the Lord can use us all! We all have shortcomings. The Lord wants to work in us and help us. I believe He will honor any efforts you make to correct your speech.

Now we need to figure out what that looks like in everyday life. Let's start with the place where we probably mess up the most. Journey with me into the place I call home. I find that it is far easier to behave and control my speech among strangers than it is with my loved ones. Since the home is where I mess up the most, that is where I decided to try to make changes first.

If you think about it, most of the negative things that come out of our mouths do not do anything to improve the situation. Our unhelpful speech only makes things worse. For example, once you have asked your spouse to do something three days in a row you start to get angry and complain. Maybe you compare your husband to the neighbor who never has an overgrown yard or your wife to your friend who always has a delicious home-cooked meal waiting on him after work. Chances are your prodding and nagging failed to get the grass cut but did succeed in growing a fight between you and your husband. Comparing yourselves to other people isn't helpful either.

Nothing is wrong with asking your spouse to do something you would like done. When it turns into fights, nagging, or snide remarks, your verbiage just failed the litmus test. It is not helpful, and it accomplishes nothing. These kinds of conversations don't benefit the other person, nor do they build them up. If anything, it does the opposite. Sometimes I want to prove my point so badly. I just don't let up. It is wrong, though, and God is dealing with my heart so that I can get better. I am trying. I want my words to say beneficial things to the people around me.

Now may be the time when most of us want to go to the back of the closet and find a pair of steel-toed boots to put on. I may be stepping on some toes with this next topic. I don't think I can address the meaning of Ephesians 4:29 and not discuss the problem of gossip. I am the world's biggest fan of minding your own business. Seriously! If I had a motto for the standard operating procedure of my life, that would be it. To a fault. I appreciate it when others mind their own business. (Sometimes that isn't good because other people need us.)

I wouldn't characterize myself as a gossip. However, gossip is one of those things that sneaks up on me. I may have no intention of talking about others to others, but before I know it, a conversation starts, and...boom, just like that, I am in the middle. Suddenly, we are talking about who said this and why "so and so" did that. How does it happen so fast? My intentions are good, yet I gossip. I don't know many people who don't gossip occasionally. It is hard not to.

Gossip is a little bit like that bag of chocolate that sits on the counter in the kitchen. You know too much chocolate is bad for you, and it is best to stay away, but each trip into the kitchen warrants another handful of yummy goodness. You know you should stay away from conversations about other people. It is the right thing to do. Then you take that trip to the copier at work, and you can't help but overhear the latest news. You want to walk away, but you do need those copies after all. You try to listen and not talk. (That is not so bad. Right?) I don't know about you, but I find it hard not to participate if I am around it. I do not go looking for gossip, but my human nature doesn't want to miss out, and I want to know what everyone else knows.

The truth is, gossip does not pass the litmus test. It doesn't benefit anyone. Neither the one talking nor the one listening. It surely does not benefit the subject of the gossip. It is unavoidable. I know we can't always stick our heads in the sand or run the other way. After all, we must use the copier at work sometimes. At lunch, our coworkers are going to talk. We can't stick our fingers in our ears and pretend not to hear. I guess the point I am making is this: Just do what you can to avoid gossip. Don't repeat it when you hear it, and when appropriate, excuse yourself from the conversation.

The book of Proverbs is one of my favorite books in the Bible. I like Proverbs because most of the time the verses are straightforward and easy to understand. The book is also full of vivid pictures and images that drive the message home. One tiny little proverb is packed with so much wisdom. I love chewing on those little morsels as I start my day.

The other day I was reading and came across a verse that draws a comparison between fire and gossip. "Without wood a fire goes out; without gossip a quarrel dies down" (Proverbs 26:20). A fire's fuel is wood. When the fuel is gone, so is the fire. A quarrel's fuel can be gossip. When the gossip is gone, the quarrel can die down. I think the lesson to be learned here is two-fold. Gossiping and talking about others only fuel problems between people. Second, letting the gossip die down can often help the dispute settle. I challenge you to take time to read through the book of Proverbs. It is full of great advice on how to handle problems and disputes with other people.

There is something else to consider that is just as important. We discussed taking time to ask if our words are beneficial to those who hear them. I want to take it a step further. King David beautifully penned the words, "May the words of my mouth and the meditation of my heart be pleasing to you, Oh Lord" (Psalms 19:14, NLT). Every now and then, I talk when nobody is listening. I might talk to myself or another person out of earshot. It is easy to use those moments to just let it rip and say whatever we want. After all, it doesn't hurt anyone if they don't hear it. The Lord always hears, and our relationship with Him is first and foremost. No loopholes here. When you talk negatively about yourself, you are not pleasing the Lord. When you mumble snide comments under your breath, that is not pleasing either. I pray this prayer daily. "Lord, help my words please You and benefit those who hear them."

Talking to Yourself

Occasionally, I talk to myself. I like to think of it as thinking out loud. I am an auditory learner, so it helps me. Sometimes it can be a conversation in my mind. Especially when emotions are running high. I recently realized that sometimes when I am talking to myself, it is not uplifting. Usually, I put myself down or convince myself that I just "can't." Why? I cannot say I know why. Negativity is contagious and grows fast. It can be a slippery slope. Once you are on the downward slide, it is hard to get your footing and make your way back up to the top.

If I am so concerned with how I talk to others, why am I not careful about what I say to myself? Shouldn't I use the same litmus test? I think I should. I think we all should. We have mostly been focusing on treating other people in the right way and being careful with our words. We are also God's creation. He loves us, and we should be careful how we talk to ourselves. One thing I try to do when I get into the habit of negative self-talk is quote Scripture. Speak God's truth over your life. Claim the promises written in Scripture. Even if you don't say these things out loud, your negative thoughts count too.

Trying to tame the tongue is difficult. I like the idea of Ephesians 4:29 as the filter for what we should and should not say. It helps me. When it comes right down to it, is what I am about to say going to be helpful? Try it for a while. I bet you will like the results. People like to be around others who respect them and are kind. This starts with the way we talk.

Chapter 6

---∝∽---

THE SOLUTION

Have you given up on me? I hope not. This is the best part. If you are like me, there have been multiple times while reading this book that you wanted to throw in the towel. Almost every time I sat down to write, I felt like it was a lost cause. Why? Because the battle is never-ending and tough. Is that the best part? No, of course not. The best part is LOVE! We have addressed what, when, where, and why. This chapter is about the how. What's love got to do with it? I'm glad you asked.

Earlier, we talked about how the Golden Rule summed up the Laws and Prophets (the Old Testament). Now let's look at the scripture that Jesus says sums it ALL up. The whole kit and caboodle. "Teacher, which is the greatest commandment in the Law? Jesus replied: 'Love the Lord your God with all your heart and with all your soul and with all your mind.' This is the first and greatest commandment. And the second is like it: 'Love your neighbor as yourself.' All the Law and the Prophets hang on these two commandments" (Matthew 22:36–40).

This is the solution to it all. It all comes down to LOVE. All those commands in the Old Testament "hang" on love. That is how you approach a relationship with the Lord and with people. The order is important too. Notice that it says to first love the Lord and then love your neighbor. It isn't easy to love others sometimes. That is precisely why I think that is the second command. First, work on loving the Lord with everything you have. Once that happens, the second part becomes a whole lot easier. Not easy, just easier.

I think the backstory of this little bit of Scripture is interesting. When Jesus began His ministry, not everyone was happy to see Him performing miracles and blessing the people. The leaders at that time were trying to trap Him and find fault with Him. That brought about one of many conversations where they would question Jesus, hoping He would incriminate Himself, or at the very least, make Himself look foolish. That never happened.

The question this time was, "Which is the greatest commandment?" Jesus, of course, did not miss a beat and used Scripture from Deuteronomy 6:5 and Leviticus 19:18 to answer them. (I highly recommend taking time to read these two passages. The one in Deuteronomy is a personal favorite of mine.) Quoting the very Scriptures these men would have known and studied, Jesus showed the answer can always be found in God's Word. Love that. You see, these men were religious leaders and knew the Scripture. I am sure they thought they would catch Him by getting Him to say some parts of Scripture were more important than others. That isn't how it went down at all. That is just how awesome the truths of Scripture are. Each verse on its own is an inspired, God-breathed Word. Together, they fit perfectly. Jesus was able to sum it all up in two short commands. 1. Love God. 2. Love people.

What Is Love?

I want to step away from the main course for a little side dish for a minute. We established that love is the solution and that we are commanded in Scripture to love others. As I was thinking about this,

I realized that love means different things to different people. When you look up the word love in the dictionary, you will notice it is both a noun and a verb. Nouns are naming words. In this case, the noun is naming the idea of love. Verbs show action. Action verbs are things that you can do. This is important because it demonstrates that love is more than an emotion or feeling. Love is an action we can and should...DO!

Merriam-Webster sums up love as strong affection or attraction for another.[8] My favorite definition from Webster is "the unselfish and loyal benevolent concern for the good of another." I love words. I can't imagine being one of the individuals who sat for endless hours defining words. What a job. What a fabulous way to describe love. We should be unselfish and loyal as we look out for the well-being of others.

If you look back at the original Greek, the Bible uses four different words for love.[9] This indicates that there are different kinds of love. The word "eros" is used to refer to romantic love. "Storge" is the word used to describe the love between family members. The word "philia" is what we call brotherly love or love between friends. It is steeped in emotion and strong bonds. This is the word you would use for your besties, your confidants, and others you care deeply for. The final and fourth word used is "agape." "Agape" love is divine. It is the perfect, unconditional, pure, and sacrificial love that Jesus demonstrated when He walked the earth. In the section below, we will talk about how we can tap into this divine love and have it flow through us. It doesn't come naturally; we need the Holy Spirit living in us to love this way.

Now, let's look at the apostle Paul's letter to the Corinthians. First Corinthians 13 is known as the love chapter. There is much to learn and digest from this scripture. I want to focus on just a few verses. Here we get a picture, or even a list, of what love is and isn't. "Love is patient, love is kind. It does not envy, it does not boast, it is not proud. It does not dishonor others, it is not self-seeking, it is not easily angered, it keeps no record of wrongs. Love does not delight in evil but rejoices with the truth. It always protects, always trusts, always hopes, always perseveres" (1 Corinthians 13:4–7).

These verses are self-explanatory. Paul shows us what love looks like. I encourage you to memorize these verses. Keep this list in the back of your mind. I have a picture of this scripture hanging in my bedroom. I do not get tired of reading it. It is like a reminder each time I see it. I need that reminder. I do not always feel like loving. Emotions can be strong. Love perseveres. Don't give up. It is not easy to show love, but stick with it. Be careful not to make the same mistake I have made in the past. At times, I think that with enough willpower and discipline, I can tame my emotions, thoughts, and tongue. I will be the first to tell you that it is a losing battle. So, what now? I believe that when we accept Jesus as our Savior, His Spirit dwells in us. As we develop a relationship with Him, we become more like Him and bear the fruits of the Spirit Galatians talks about (more on that later). We need to be rooted and grounded in our relationship with the Lord first, and the rest follows suit.

STAY CONNECTED

In the book of John, Jesus refers to Himself as the vine. We, His followers, are the branches. Let's take a minute and let that marinate. It will help us with this solution to the bully incognito. Love is the answer. I know it sounds so very cliché, but it happens to be true.

My thumbs are not green and probably never will be. Gardening, or keeping plants alive in general, just isn't a talent or passion of mine. One thing I do know is that if the branch is cut away from the vine or tree, it loses its life source. Hence, the branch dies. I have a Gerber daisy planted in my front yard. I claim it will survive a nuclear attack. I give it little to no attention, yet it thrives. It produces a crazy number of flowers in the spring and fall, but the moment I cut the daisies to adorn the kitchen table, they start to die. The plant doesn't die. It has roots, and its life source remains intact. The flower is no longer connected with the roots and will not receive what it needs to keep living.

This is the picture painted in John 15:1–17. In verse 5 Jesus says, "I am the vine; you are the branches. If a man remains in me and I in him, he will bear much fruit; apart from me you can do nothing." We must bear fruit. There are several fruits of God's spirit mentioned in Galatians 5:22–23. The one we are focusing on here is love. If we are connected with our Lord, we will be able to produce fruit. We will be able to love others. Sure, there will be droughts. Other branches will crowd our space or soak up our sunlight. The good news is that our vine will never wither or die. We always have a source of life. We are not without help. Loving God and people is work, but it is our greatest command to follow. Stay connected to the vine. Your life depends on it.

It should be evident that we are Christians. We will be known by our love. If we stay connected to the vine and "remain in" Jesus, we will bear fruit. It is a cause-and-effect scenario. One is the natural result of the other. We can't rely on our human nature because we will fail. Sometimes people annoy me or make me mad. I don't want to love them. My feelings get in the way. If I am bearing the fruits of the spirit by having a relationship with Jesus, His nature will shine through. The Holy Spirit can then work in and through us. Thank goodness. That is an encouragement to me.

Before Jesus was crucified, He tried to tell his disciples that He would not be with them for very much longer. He did not keep His coming death a secret. The disciples loved Jesus and were prepared to follow Him anywhere. Peter promised to lay down his life for Jesus, and he eventually did. Peter suffered from a lack of tongue control, like many of us. I love reading about Peter. I relate to him. He made huge mistakes, yet he was the rock the church was built upon. While Peter is promising to follow Jesus even if it means death, we come across yet another command from Jesus. "A NEW command I give you. Love one another. As I have loved you, so you must love one another. By this everyone will know you are my disciples if you love one another" (John 13:34–35). You see, we are marked as followers of Jesus by the love that shines through us.

Now, if you know the story of Peter, then you know he fails to keep his promise at first and even denies that he knew Jesus. To be honest, I cannot say I would have done much better. Those were scary times. Peter was restored and is a great example of how to follow Jesus with reckless abandon and passion. I imagine Peter felt awful after denying Jesus. He was not left that way, though.

Jesus appeared to Peter after His resurrection. While Peter is fishing, he comes ashore to see Jesus cooking breakfast. I love the picture here. The God of the universe is partaking of everyday meals, and not only that, but ministering to His beloved disciples while doing it. Jesus asked Peter three times if he loved Him, and three times Peter assured Jesus that he did. Two things to note: One, Jesus asked three times to restore Peter after the three times Peter denied knowing Jesus. Second, the word Jesus uses here is "agape." Remember, that is divine love. Peter responds with Phila, or brotherly love, but the story does not end there. After Jesus ascends into heaven, His disciples are given the task of spreading the good news about Jesus. You can read in Acts about how the Holy Spirit comes to the new believers, just as promised by Jesus. It is no accident that Jesus used the word "agape." If Peter can be called to love Jesus's sheep, or people, with an agape love, so can we.

Jesus wanted the disciples to change their focus from simply following Him around as friends and helpers to going into the world and showing God's love. That is exactly what we are meant to do. People will know we are different because we bear the fruit of God's love. It isn't natural; it is spiritual. The average person wants to fit in and be one of the gang. We don't typically like to appear different. I include myself in that category. The truth is that if we have a relationship with the Lord and share His love, then we will stand out. The Bible says the world may even hate us because of Jesus. That is all right with me. It is worth it to let His love shine through me.

Love is the solution, because that is how we will be able to curtail the urges of our human nature when it comes to how we talk to others. It is much easier to treat someone the way we should when we love them the way Jesus would. We have been given not only the gift of eternal life but also one of unconditional love. The closest thing I could imagine likening God's love to is the love between a parent and a child. It would have to be even better because it is perfect love. Human parents can't be perfect, but that is still the closest thing to unconditional love I can think of on this earth. I tell my girls all the time that I will love them no matter what.

My prayer for you is that you find comfort in knowing that nothing can separate you from God's love. Absolutely nothing can come between you and your heavenly Father's love. You cannot earn it. It isn't possible. God will not hold it over your head or guilt you with it. His love is there for us all, and it is up to us to tap into it. We have free will. With that comes the ability to either accept the gift of salvation and God's love or to turn away from it. Romans tells us to confess with our mouths that we believe Jesus to be the Savior of the world who died and rose again and who will return one day for His people. There is not a magical prayer or a specific verse to recite. It is a heart matter. If you believe and confess that belief, you can experience salvation and eternal life with Jesus in heaven.

Love is what will help us when we are in situations where we want to let it rip. People can mistreat us and hurt us. We don't want to love them back. We want to let them have it. I get it. That is why we need Jesus's love running through us. The moment I rely on my own capacity for love, I am doomed to mess up. That tank will empty quickly. If I spend time with the Lord and allow His love to work through me, I can count on God's help to love the seemingly unlovable.

One of my all-time favorite devotionals is *My Utmost for His Highest* by Oswald Chambers.[10] On April 30, the message is titled "Spontaneous Love." Oswald Chambers says this: "It (love) burst forth in extraordinary ways. We don't deliberately set the statements before us as our standard, but when His Spirit is having His way with us, we live according to His standard without even realizing it." If we allow God to work in us, His nature will take over and the love will be spontaneous. It will come naturally. That is my prayer. I am not there yet, but I am working on it.

Chambers concludes his message for that day by saying, "The fountains from which love flow are in God, not in us." We need God's love to work in us and through us if we are to be successful in taming this bully incognito. Romans 5:5 says it this way, "And hope does not disappoint us, because God has poured out His love into our hearts through the Holy Spirit, whom He has given us" (BSB). God's Word tells us that we have God's love poured into us. One piece of Scripture that I regularly pray over my family is from Ephesians 3:16–20. I hope that if my family and I learn to "be rooted" in God's love that "surpasses all understanding," we will be able to show God's love so naturally that others see the Lord and not us.

Chapter 7

---∞---

THE CHALLENGE

At this point, it may seem like you are riding a sinking ship because we are all human, and there is no way we can keep our tongue in check one hundred percent of the time. I agree that it is difficult, and we WILL mess up. Some of us will struggle more than others, but we will all let it slip at some point. I am sure it is impossible not to. Do not lose heart just yet. God's forgiveness and grace are there for us when we need it. However, the Bible does tell us that if we love God, we will not want to offend Him with our sins. Try to pull back on those reins and slow down. I think you will see a big improvement.

Sincere love is the antidote to snide remarks and a combative tongue. If we truly love as we are called to love each other, then we will be able to keep our human nature in check. It is hard to speak nicely to people we do not love. Let's face it. Some people are just downright hard to be around. They rub you the wrong way, step on your toes, or do any number of things that get in the way of you loving them. Sincere love can't be faked. If I don't care for you, chances are it shows. I don't hide it very well. Some of us may be better actors than others, but truth always finds its way out. If we love like God loves, it will be real, sincere, and true. We must love before we can fix our words.

A Heart Problem

When we spend time with God, study His Word, and pray, it will show in our daily actions or "fruit." Remember, earlier we discussed that "out of the mouth the heart speaks." You see, it is as much a heart problem as a problem with our words. If we go to the "heart" of the issue, we will have the advantage in this battle. The adage "garbage in, garbage out" is very true. When we fill our eyes, ears, and minds with negativity, it will seep into our hearts and wait to be regurgitated through our words. What now? How do we cut the words off from the source? We need a change of heart. Thoughts become words, and words become actions. What we think about matters.

The book of Philippians has a gold mine of scripture nuggets that are perfect for encouraging and strengthening your faith. Philippians 4:8–9 addresses our thoughts. These verses remind us to think about things that are true, noble, right, pure, lovely, admirable, excellent, and praiseworthy. That is a long list of good things to think about. If your thoughts don't line up with this list, the words that follow will probably not pass the litmus test we spoke about in chapter 5.

Of course, we will have times when the words slip out before we can catch them, but they do not have to get the best of us. In 2 Peter 1:4, we are promised and encouraged that we can be marked and "participate in God's nature." Because His spirit lives in us, we can bear fruit such as love and self-control that will allow us to be better managers of the tiny, but powerful, rudder that steers the vessels we call our bodies.

You can also replace unwanted thoughts with Scripture. I challenge you to try. Memorize God's Word. In Psalms 119:11 David writes, "I have hidden Your word in my heart that I might not sin against You." Put God's Word in your heart, and that is what will come out. There is no special formula or prayer we need to recite. I know that I am guilty of trying to do things on my own accord and in my own power. The harder I try, the harder I fail. No kidding. When I try to do the right thing and let my pride take over, failure is usually not far behind. I doubt I am alone here. (At least I hope not.) It can be very discouraging to work hard at something and still come up short. I am here to tell you from experience that if you don't recognize your need for help, you won't get very far. We are created by God to glorify Him. The same void He fills in us through His salvation is the void He fills in us as we develop a relationship with Him.

Do you have a person in your life that you are close to? After spending hours, days, months, and even years with them, you turn around and realize that you have taken on some of their habits and characteristics. Right? I think that is great. We influence the people we are around, and they influence us. You cannot have relationships without influence. We can have a relationship with the Creator of the universe, and He can influence us in a tangible way. Take my challenge to develop that relationship while keeping tabs on your tongue. The two go hand in hand. It will be impossible to tackle the mighty tongue without tapping into God's power.

Jesus told us that he would send the Holy Spirit to help us and guide us. When you know God and have a relationship with Him. His very power can work through you. You can do this. Sure, you will mess up, and some days you will not even believe what just came out of your mouth. Don't be too hard on yourself, and don't expect perfection.

Let me talk about one more aspect of this whole bully incognito that I haven't mentioned yet. That is forgiveness. I read this story about a professor who gave her students a surprise test in class one day. My first thought was that it was harsh. Especially in college. Tests are brutal. Her idea fascinated me, though. The students were asked to complete one task. They were to turn their paper over and write about what they observed on the page. What was on the page? One tiny black dot and nothing else was in the center of the page. How do you even start? What is there to say? Well, of course, the students wrote as they were instructed to do.

At the end of class, the professor had the students share their writing. She made this observation. Everyone wrote about the black dot, and not one single person addressed all the white space around it. Her objective was to make this point. We do the same thing in life. We focus on one tiny aspect and forget all of the "white space" around it. I was thinking about it a couple of days later, and I thought that relationships are a little like this lesson. Sometimes relationships get black dots. People hurt us. It gets hard to focus on the whole picture. There was more to that page than the black dot. There is more to our relationships than the offenses people commit against us. It is all about perspective and what you choose to focus on. It is a choice.

No person can earn forgiveness. We don't even deserve it. Forgiveness is a gift. You give it away and expect nothing in return. There are no gift receipts or return lines. It is nonrefundable. God modeled this forgiveness in many ways. Jesus even prayed for forgiveness for the men who were crucifying him. My mind cannot even wrap itself around that. Because of Jesus's sacrifice, we have forgiveness and access to God and heaven. Without forgiveness, we would be doomed. We cannot earn our way to eternal life in heaven. It was given to us. All we must do is receive and accept it.

People will hurt you. They will make you mad and do things you think are wrong. We need to forgive them. It will go against everything in our being. Our nature will resist. That is where that relationship with Jesus comes into play. It isn't just our efforts that get us there. We have help. When Jesus taught His disciples to pray, one of the lines included in His example prayer was "Forgive us our debts and we forgive our debtors." It is a two-way street. You see, we will also mess up and hurt others. We will make them mad or do something to hurt them. On that day, we will want forgiveness too.

I find myself getting discouraged sometimes when I let my words get away from me and say something I shouldn't. I like to remind myself that it is an uphill battle and won't be won in a day. I was reading Galatians 5:16–26, and Paul is talking about the struggle between our spirit and flesh. He mentions this in more than one of his letters. He tells us they want what is contrary to each other. Paul tells us that if we are led by the Spirit, we can "crucify our sinful nature with its passions and desires." We talked about the fruit of the Spirit earlier.

If we surrender our sinful nature and let God's nature take over, we will find it a little easier each day to fight this battle of the bully incognito. Remember, we cannot escape God's love. Romans 8:38–39 says it this way. "For I am convinced that neither death nor life, neither angels nor demons, neither the present nor the future, nor any powers, neither height nor depth nor anything else in all creation, will be able to separate us from the love of God that is in Christ Jesus our Lord." We will mess up, fail, and then pick it all back up again. That is okay. Do not give up. No matter what, we can't escape God's love.

I think it is also important to note that we can show our love for God through obedience. Give it your best shot while remembering that it is not by our strength but our success in battling this bully incognito will be because of the Lord's help. Maybe some of you think you are too far gone. God's forgiveness is for us all. On those days when it gets rough and you mess up, remember this verse. "Create in me a pure heart, O God, and renew a steadfast spirit within me" (Psalm 51:10). We may have strayed and become bitter, but God can renew our hearts.

It is also important to remember that you are not the only one who struggles. We all must work daily. It helps me to know I'm not the only one. More importantly, God is there with us on this journey. We may not always feel Him. Have faith. He is for you and will bless your efforts to obey His Word. Remember the declarative sentence? Remember Ephesians 4:29? "Let no unwholesome talk come out of your mouth." It is not a suggestion but an instruction. I pray for God's blessing as you follow the instructions in His holy Word.

One final thought. I have talked quite a bit about how much damage our words can do, and it is true. They can. I don't want to end there. The thing I want to leave you with is this. Words can have the same power to accomplish positive results. Proverbs says, "The tongue has the power of life and death, and those who love it will eat its fruit" (Proverbs 18:21). The consequences of our words can also be positive.

In science, we learn that for every action there is an equal and opposite reaction. We tend to think of consequences as being negative, but that isn't always the case. Positive behaviors and actions produce positive consequences. That means our words have just as much power to do good as they do to harm. Just like gossip can fuel the fire or quarrel between people, our words can fuel a very different kind of fire. Be the spark that ignites and fuels fires of love and kindness in your home, the workplace, and even the grocery store.

My prayer is that you will have the faith to believe you can change, the hope to get you through the tough days when you mess up, and the love for those around you to help you speak life into the lives of others.

Chapter 8

―――――∞―――――

QUICK HELP/VERSES
TO MEMORIZE

One thing that can help in the journey and fight against the "bully incognito" is to memorize God's Word. We are instructed to "hide God's word in our heart that we might not sin against Him" (Psalm 119:11). We learned that "out of the overflow of the heart the mouth speaks" (Luke 6:45). If God's Word is in our heart, then that is what will come out of our mouth. Pick a verse from below at the beginning of the week. Memorize the scripture and say the prayer included, or better yet, see what God is speaking to your heart and come up with a prayer of your own. You can repeat this section as many times as needed. You can even focus on a verse for longer than a week. I also would not be surprised that as you pray and walk with the Lord, He reveals new scriptures and ideas unique to your needs and situations. I am praying for you.

A gentle answer turns away wrath, but a harsh word stirs up anger.

Proverbs 15:1

The adage that you "attract more flies with honey than vinegar" is so true. My automatic reaction when someone speaks to me in a way I don't like is to respond in a curt, rude, or firm tone. This scripture advises us to do the exact opposite. Rather than responding with the tangy and pungent kick of vinegar, add some sweet honey to your tone. The next time someone is letting you have it or treating you unkindly, fight the urge to respond the same way. Watch in amazement when you reply with a "gentle answer" and in love. Chances are, they will not even know what to do next. Most of the time, it will disarm them completely. Of course, there are exceptions. Don't let that stop you. I have seen it in action.

Person "A" is fired up and ready to go. Verbal bullets are loaded. Next, person "B" won't play the game. They refuse to respond in the same way. Instead, they stay calm and gentle to reply in God's love. Boom! Just like that, the "wrath" begins to diminish. The results are way better than any zinger would have yielded. Suddenly, a verbal exchange is not as enticing when the other person will not engage. Try it! You may just avoid conflict. This verse applies to our everyday life. I believe it with all my heart. If you are not genuine with your "honey" responses, the other person may see right through it. It works best if our interactions and verbal exchanges are rooted in God's love.

Don't forget the second part of the verse. It is equally as effective. If you respond (or initiate) with "harsh words," anger is going to follow. I think of it as a chemistry lab. In your beaker, you have the other person's emotions, feelings, and responses. In flask one, you have your "gentle answer." In flask two, you hold your "harsh word." If you unload flask two's contents, make sure you are wearing your goggles. There is bound to be an unpleasant reaction.

Dear Lord,

Thank You for being with me when others mistreat me or make me angry. Help me not to sin in my frustration and anger. I want to respond with gentle answers and not wrath. It isn't my nature, so I will need help. When people come against me with harshness and anger, give me the strength to follow Your Word and turn the situation around with gentleness. In Jesus's name, I pray. Amen.

> *And God is able to make all grace abound to you, so that in all things, at all times, having all you need, you will abound in every good work (BSB).*

> 2 Corinthians 9:8

Do not be discouraged when you mess up. (There are no "ifs" here. We will all mess up). God's grace is there for us. Extend grace to yourself and those around you when unkind words slip. The last part of the verse is great. You can "abound in every good work," and trying to get a handle on the way we use our words is good work. God will bless your efforts if you ask Him.

Dear Lord,

Forgive me when my words don't glorify You and show Your love. I want to bear Your fruit. I want others to know that I am Your child by the way I speak and act. When I make mistakes, help me to know that I can be forgiven and that grace is waiting for me. Help me to extend this same grace to others. Thank You for Your grace. Amen.

Set a guard over my mouth, O Lord; Keep watch over the door of my lips (NRSV).

Psalm 141:3

This is just a great verse to memorize. It is a short, simple prayer great for those moments when you have had enough. God's Word is referred to as a sword. We can do battle with God's Word. When you think you can't do it anymore, pray this prayer, and then know that God is there for you as you work on this. We get tired. God does not. I like the image of asking Him, the Almighty Lord, to keep watch over the door of our lips. Sometimes we leave doors open, and then other times we keep them shut. Just like our lips. It is a good comparison. Ask God to help you determine when and where you speak. Ask Him to keep this prayer in the forefront of your mind for when things really get hard. He is faithful.

Dear Lord,

Give me strength when the challenges of life cause my emotions to rise and things get heated. Help my mouth and words be guarded. Help me today as I close my lips to keep unkind words in. May I look to You and renew my thinking when tough times come. Thank You for keeping watch over me and the door to my lips. Thank You for being the strength in my weakness. I love You, Lord. Amen.

May these words of my mouth and this meditation of my heart be pleasing in your sight, O Lord, my Rock and my Redeemer.

Psalm 19:14

Earlier, we discussed how what is in our hearts will eventually seep out of our mouths. Often, our thoughts become words, and then those words become actions. If our "meditations" are on things of God, our words are more likely to be on the up and up. What we concentrate on and think about matters. We can be intentional about our thoughts and discipline them just like we discipline ourselves in other areas. If we are thinking about the right things, it will help us say the right things.

Dear Lord,

Today, I ask You to help me keep track of my words. Let them be acceptable and pleasing to You, Lord, above all else. May it start with my meditations and thoughts. Guide me as I work to keep my thoughts on the right things and look to you. Amen.

> *Finally, brothers and sisters, whatever is true, whatever is noble, whatever is right, whatever is pure, whatever is lovely, whatever is admirable—if anything is excellent or praiseworthy—think about such things.*
>
> Philippians 4:8

This is a continuation of the ideas from the last verse. They go together. Remember that what comes out of our mouths is the overflow of our thoughts and what is in our hearts. Are you thinking on the things of this world, or are you thinking on things that honor God? This is a great scripture to memorize and a good reminder that what goes on in the quiet places of our hearts is important too. The more we think about the right things, the easier it will be to say the right things.

Dear Lord,

Today, I am asking You to help me with my thoughts. I want to correct my thinking. I want to think of the things that are lovely and pure. Help me to hide Your Word in my heart and apply it to my daily walk. When negativity or wrong thinking creeps in, help me to remember Your Word and think about things that honor You. Even when it seems like I cannot do it, be with me, Lord, as I seek to glorify You. Amen

> *Love is patient, love is kind. It does not envy, it does not boast, it is not proud. It does not dishonor others, it is not self-seeking, it is not easily angered, it keeps no record of wrongs. Love does not delight in evil but rejoices with the truth. It always protects, always trusts, always hopes, always perseveres.*
>
> 1 Corinthians 13:4–7

This is a list of what love is and is not. Refer to it when you need help. Those moments when your neighbor, family member, or even you are difficult to love. Quote these verses and be strengthened by God's Word. Real progress can be made in relationships when you are not easily angered and don't keep records of wrongdoing. I like to read this verse and challenge myself to reflect and think about how I love those around me.

Dear Lord,

Thank You for being patient with me as I learn to love others and speak the way You would have me speak. Help me to be unselfish and see others through Your eyes. Jesus, You are our example of how love should be lived out. Make me a disciple of Your love. It will not make sense by the world's standards, and others may find me strange, but let Your love be the first thing others see in me. Amen.

My dear brothers and sisters, take note of this: Everyone should be quick to listen, slow to speak and slow to become angry, because human anger does not produce the righteousness that God desires.

James 1:19–20:

So many arguments are caused simply by miscommunication. There are times when I am talking to people, and I notice myself thinking about my next response rather than listening. Maybe you do that too. It is especially true if I am upset. If we listen first, we might learn something from the other person. This verse puts listening before talking, and it warns against anger. We are more likely to sin when we are angry. Something I tell my kids and students is that we have two eyes, two ears, and only one mouth. This suggests we should look and listen twice as much as we speak. It may seem silly, but it is a good visual to help us think about how we interact with people. We will learn more about the people and the world around us if we use our eyes and ears before our mouths.

Dear Lord,

Please help me to be a good listener. When I feel like I have something to say, help me to be patient and hear the other person first. I want to be slow to speak and more careful with my responses. I don't want to respond in anger. When I am upset, help me to remember Your Word and slow down. I want others to know that I care and am interested in their needs and feelings, rather than just thinking about what I have to say. Thank You, Lord, for Your blessing and guidance. Amen.

> *Whoever of you loves life and desires to see many good days, keep your tongue from evil and your lips from telling lies. Turn from evil and do good; seek peace and pursue it.*
>
> Psalm 34:12–14

Telling lies can devastate your relationships. Trust is a vital part of your relationships with other people. If your loved ones, or even coworkers, can't trust you, it is hard to have a healthy relationship. Trust can be broken in many ways, but we are focusing on words. It hurts when someone lies to us. It causes us to keep our guard up around the person who lied to us because we don't want to get hurt again. In the back of our minds, we are wondering when the next lie will come. The verses tell us that if we love life and want to see "many good days," we need to tell the truth and keep our tongue from evil. We can make improvements in our speech and relationships by being truthful.

Dear Lord,

Thank You for another day to serve You. Forgive me for any lies or evil speech I am guilty of. Bring to my mind those I have hurt with my words and lies. I pray for the restoration of those relationships. I know it may take time. I am willing to start fresh. I want to be truthful and honest with everyone I encounter today. I want to build trust that is based on the foundation of truth. Amen.

> *The tongue has the power of life and death, and those who love it will eat its fruits.*

Proverbs 18:21

This verse lays it out clearly. Words are powerful and can even be the difference between life and death. To some, it may seem extreme. One of the things that came to mind when I was thinking about this verse relates to World War II and the Holocaust. Adolf Hitler became the dictator of Germany. One strategy he used to rise to power and then annihilate the Jews was propaganda, or words. Many lost their lives during the Holocaust because Hitler's words were powerful.

There is a translation of the Bible called The Message that phrases things very simply. In this version, the verse reads, "Words kill, words give life; they're either poison or fruit—you choose" (MSG). The choice is up to us. What will we accomplish with our words? This also makes me think about reaping and sowing. The words we plant will produce the consequences we harvest. If we sow words of life around us, then that is the harvest we will reap. That encourages me. I like the thought of speaking life into those around me.

Dear Lord,

I want to give You all the praise. You alone are worthy. I want to choose my words wisely. I pray that what I say will give life and not bring death. Encourage me as I take on this challenge. May my words and actions please You today. In Jesus's holy name, I pray. Amen.

And whatever you do, whether in word or deed, do it all in the name of the Lord Jesus, giving thanks to God the Father through him.

Colossians 3:17

We are here for God's glory. We want our actions and words to point others to Him. No matter how small the task, we give honor to our Lord. God uses the small things. He will bless your efforts to honor Him with your words. Don't give up on this journey to control your tongue. It will not be a success story every day. God will not leave you to do it alone. We can't do it alone. Just keep focusing on the right things, and remember that it is worth the work and effort.

Dear Lord,

Thank You for giving me life. May I always remember that I am here to give You glory and honor. May the words I speak and my actions be in Your name. All that I do, I do in the name of Jesus, that He may be glorified. Help me on this journey, as it is not something I can accomplish once and move on. I will need You daily. Today, I pray others see Jesus through me. Amen.

A NEW command I give you. Love one another. As I have loved you, so you must love one another. By this everyone will know you are my disciples, if you love one another.

John 13:34–35

I am not sure I can even imagine what it would have been like to be one of the people to walk the earth with Jesus. Even just a passerby on the streets of Jerusalem. It must have been something to witness Him in person. The Bible says we will be blessed for believing without seeing. We can also be Jesus's disciples. As we emulate Him and live our lives through faith, we can be disciples.

Jesus explains to His followers that there is a new command. It is all about love. He knew He was going to be crucified, rise from the dead, and forty days later ascend into heaven. He set the example. We are to follow that example. Loving people in Jesus's way did not fit the political or spiritual norms of His day. It seemed strange to those observing Him and even angered the religious leaders. If we love others the way He loves us, it may not seem natural to others, but it is our command to follow. Be disciples of His love. Spread it to those around you. Your words will fall in line, and your love will grow.

Dear Lord,

I am eternally grateful for Your love. I don't deserve it even on my best days. I want to learn to love others the way You love me. As I read Your Word, pray, and spend time with You, help me to be a disciple of Your love. My prayer is that others will see You in me. I want Your love to be evident when I interact with others. Help my words demonstrate Your love. I give You all the glory and praise. Amen.

ENDNOTES

1. Introduction: What is the Bully Incognito

The Editors of Encyclopaedia Britannica. 2019. "Logos | Philosophy and Theology | Britannica." In *Encyclopædia Britannica*. https://www.britannica.com/topic/logos.

2. Pfeiffer, Charles F., and Everett Falconer Harrison. 1990. *The Wycliffe Bible Commentary*. Chicago: Moody Publishers.

Chapter One: The Problem

3. Chapman, Gary D. 2010. *The Five Love Languages: How to Express Heartfelt Commitment to Your Mate*. Nashville, TN: Lifeway Press.

Chapter Two: The War Zone

4. "Definition of NICE." 2017. Merriam-Webster.com. 2017. https://www.merriam-webster.com/dictionary/nice.

5. "Definition of KIND." n.d. Www.merriam-Webster.com. https://www.merriam-webster.com/dictionary/kind.

6. "Definition of Kind | Dictionary.com." 2019. Www.dictionary.com. 2019. https://www.dictionary.com/browse/kind.

Chapter Three: The Plank Eye Phenomenon

7. Lewis, C. S. 2001. *Mere Christianity: A Revised and Amplified Edition, with a New Introduction, of the Three Books, Broadcast Talks, Christian Behaviour, and beyond Personality*. HarperCollins ed. San Francisco: Harper San Francisco.

Chapter Six: The Solution

8. Merriam-Webster. 2024. "Definition of LOVE." Merriam-Webster.com. 2024. https://www.merriam-webster.com/dictionary/love.

9. Zavada, Jack. "4 Types of Love in the Bible." Learn Religions, Feb. 8, 2021, learnreligions.com/types-of-love-in-the-bible-700177.

10. Oswald Chambers. 1992. *My Utmost for His Highest*. Grand Rapids, Mich.: Discovery House.